Gofors & Grumps

Book three

M-S

An A-Z of Bible Characters by **Derek Prime**

with illustrations by **Ruth Goodridge**

DayOnepublications

Copyright © Derek Prime 1995
First printed 1995

ISBN   0 902548 59 X

Published by Day One Publications
6 Sherman Road, Bromley, Kent BR1 3JH

Designed by Steve Devane and printed by Clifford Frost Ltd, Wimbledon SW19 2SE

Gofors & Grumps
M-S

DayOnepublications

Mr **Magic**

Magic is the power to do clever tricks that people cannot usually do. In many parts of the world, especially in some of the forests where Indian tribes live, witch-doctors practise magic; and so too do people called witches.

Magic is a word we also use to describe what magicians do.

Have you been to a birthday party where a conjuror did tricks that amazed you? You have probably wondered how he did them!

Conjurors' magic is not really magic. They are clever with their hands, and they know how to make us think something is happening when it is not!

Unfortunately, some people believe in magic, and in spells. They often wear charms around their necks or have them as bracelets.

Lots of people read their horoscopes in the newspaper. They think that what is going to happen to them in the future depends on the date of their birthday and the position of the stars.

Some men and women will never walk under a ladder, or allow you to cross the knives when you are getting out the cutlery to lay a table.

Others will go to a fair and pay a fortune teller to tell them their fortunes, or the palmist to read

Our Bible dictionary

Satan

Satan is another name for the devil.

He is against all that is good, and he is behind everything that is evil in the world. He brought men and women under his power by tempting Adam and Eve to disobey God so that they and we deserve to die and to be separated from God.

The Bible does not explain why God allowed Satan to have such power, but it tells us the good news that the Lord Jesus came into the world as a human being so that He could break Satan's power: the Lord Jesus did this when He died on the Cross as the Substitute for sinners, and then rose again.

When the Lord Jesus returns, all Satan's power will be taken away from him for ever.

their hands and tell them what is going to happen in the future.

Bookshops sell books about magic, and some people, including children, foolishly play with ouija boards.

In a ouija board the letters of the alphabet are arranged in a semi-circle with the words 'yes' or 'no' at either end. Then a glass is turned upside down and people place a finger on the glass asking a spirit to move the glass. They treat ouija as a game, but really it is dangerous and wrong.

There is nothing wrong with conjurors' magic if they only want to entertain us, and make us guess how they do the clever things they do. Many of us like doing tricks and puzzles. But magic is wrong when people believe in it, and allow it to tell them what to do.

Satan, our great enemy, is behind all the magic people believe in. He does not want people to trust in God but to trust in him instead.

Magic goes back a long time. Right at the beginning of the Bible, God told His people that they were not to imitate the horrible things they saw other nations do. No one was to do magic by the power of evil spirits. They were not to cast spells, or to try to be in touch with people who were dead. Anyone who does such things displeases God.

Sometimes people talk about 'Black Magic', and that is magic where men and women deliberately call upon the devil either to worship him or to ask him to do things for them.

The real name of Mr. Magic in the Bible was Simon. He lived in Samaria in the first century.

Christians had arrived in Samaria when they had had to leave Jerusalem when they were persecuted. They immediately told the good news of Jesus to the people there. One of those Christians was Philip.

The people of Samaria had never heard the good news about Jesus before. Not only did Philip preach about Jesus, but God gave him power to perform miracles in the name of Jesus.

The Samaritans listened carefully to what Philip said, and saw the miracles he did. Evil spirits made a loud noise as they came out of many demon-possessed people. Those who were paralysed or crippled were healed. There was great joy in the city.

Simon had practised magic for a long time in Samaria. He was really famous for his magic and he cast all kinds of spells.

He boasted that he was someone great, and everyone admired him, and said, 'This man has great power!'

But when people believed the good news Philip

Something to do

Mark the map!
Find where Samaria, the Gaza Desert and Ethiopia are on the maps on pages 46 and 47 and write in their names

Our Bible dictionary

Persecute, Persecution
To persecute is to treat people cruelly and unfairly usually because of what they believe. From the beginning Christians have often been persecuted because of their faith. See what the Lord Jesus says in John 15:20,21. Persecution of Christians still happens in many parts of the world.

brought about the Lord Jesus, they stopped taking any notice of Simon. Soon Simon said that he believed in Jesus.

Simon followed Philip everywhere, and was amazed at the great signs and miracles Philip could do, without any of the magic and tricks Simon always used.

Two of the apostles - Peter and John - came down to Samaria to see what God had been doing through Philip. Simon, Mr. Magic, saw the great power that God had given them too through His Holy Spirit. He then did something foolish and silly. He offered Peter and John money if they would give him the power they had!

God's power cannot be bought with money. God gives His Holy Spirit to those who trust in the Lord Jesus, and who want to live to please Him.

Peter told off Simon right away. 'May your money die with you,' he said, 'because you thought you could buy God's gift of His Spirit with money. Your heart is not right before God. Repent of this wickedness and pray for God's forgiveness. Perhaps he will forgive you for having such a thought in your heart. I can see there is jealousy and sin in your heart.'

'Please pray for me,' Simon asked, 'so that the bad things you have said may not happen to me'.

Christians do not have to do silly things like 'touching wood', or keeping their fingers crossed, or avoiding walking under ladders. We do not have to be afraid of magic or of Satan because the Lord Jesus has overcome all the powers of evil for us. When He rose again from the dead, He was victorious over Satan and all evil powers.

The lesson of Mr. Magic, Simon, is that we should not have anything to do with magic, but trust in the Lord Jesus and in Him alone. When we trust in Him, we do not need to be afraid of anything or anyone!

Where to read: Acts 8:4-24; Deuteronomy 18:9-13

Mr **Nobody**

If we call someone a 'nobody' we are saying that he or she is not very important. A 'somebody' is a person whom everyone takes notice of, like a King or Queen, or a Prime Minister or President, or an international footballer or tennis player.

When Mr. and Miss Somebody arrive at an airport or railway station, important people go out to meet them, and a red carpet is put down.

But when Mr. Nobody arrives, no one takes any notice, and no preparations are made to welcome him.

A wonderful truth the Bible teaches is that no one is a 'nobody' to God. Everyone is important to Him!

When the Lord Jesus was here on earth, He showed that little children or beggars in the street are as important to God as kings and queens, prime ministers, presidents and politicians.

Perhaps you feel sometimes that you are a nobody? As you come in the front door of your home, maybe your father asks your mother, 'Who is that?' 'Oh, nobody,' she answers. And she then tells him that it is only you!

Let me tell you about Mr. Nobody. That name was given to him at least twice. The first time was when an important visitor came to his home while he was out in the fields looking after his father's sheep.

At that time King Saul was king over Israel. He had failed to please God as a king, and God was going to choose another ruler for the people. God's servant - a

man called Samuel - was sent by God to the home of Jesse because one of Jesse's sons was to be the next king.

Samuel asked Jesse to bring all his sons to meet him. Jesse did so with just one son missing. Can you guess who it was he did not call to come to meet Samuel? Yes, someone whom he thought was Mr. Nobody, his youngest son, David.

Since David was his youngest son, who spent his time looking after his father's sheep, Jesse did not think it important for Samuel to meet him.

One by one Jesse's sons were introduced to Samuel, until all seven of the eight had been brought to him. Samuel was puzzled, because he knew that the Lord had not chosen any one of them.

So Samuel asked Jesse, 'Are these all the sons you have?'

'There is the youngest,' replied Jesse, 'but he is looking after the sheep.'

Samuel said, 'Send for him straightaway. We will not sit down and eat until he arrives.'

So Jesse sent for David, and introduced him to Samuel. He looked a healthy and strong young man. Then the Lord said to Samuel, 'This is the one!'

The youngest son whom everyone thought was a nobody God made into a somebody!

Not long afterwards the same thing happened again! David continued to look after his sheep because it was still a secret that he was to be the next king.

A war was going on between Israel and the Philistines, and three of David's brothers joined Saul's army to fight against them.

The Philistines had a great champion fighter called Goliath. He was over nine feet tall, and everyone looked small besides him.

He had a strong helmet on his head, and wore a suit of armour. On his legs he wore bronze leggings, and a javelin was slung on his back.

He carried a huge spear, and its iron point was large and strong. Ahead of him went his shield-bearer.

All the men of Israel's army were afraid of him. Goliath stood and shouted at them, 'Why do our whole armies fight? Am I not a Philistine, and are you not servants of Saul? Choose a man and have him come and fight me. If he is able to kill me, we will become your subjects. But if I overcome him and kill him, you will become our subjects and serve us.' Then he said, 'Today I challenge all the soldiers of Israel! Give me a man, and let us fight each other.'

As soon as Saul's soldiers heard this they were terrified, including David's brothers.

At this time Jesse, David's father, sent David to visit his brothers to find out how they were and to take them some food.

Early in the morning, David left his sheep with another shepherd, loaded up all the food he was to take, and did as his father had told him.

He reached the army camp just as Goliath came out

again and repeated his challenge. When the soldiers saw Goliath, they ran away.

David's brothers were cross and rude when they found him waiting for them at their tents. 'Why have you come here?' his oldest brother asked. 'You have just come down to watch the battle.'

That was not true because it was David's father who had told him to visit his brothers. But David took no notice. Instead he went to King Saul and said, 'Don't give in to Goliath. I'll go and fight him!'

You can guess, I expect, what was in Saul's mind. 'You are a nobody!' was what Saul thought. He said, 'You are only a boy, and Goliath has been a fighting man since he was a youth.'

David replied, 'Your servant has been looking after his father's sheep. When a lion and a bear came and carried off sheep from the flock, I went after them, struck them, and rescued the sheep from their mouth. When they turned on me, I seized them by their hair, and killed them. Your servant has killed both the lion and the bear. The same will happen to this Philistine because he has defied the armies of the living God.'

He then added, 'The Lord who delivered me from the paw of the lion and the paw of the bear will deliver me from the hand of this Philistine.'

Saul had no answer to what David said. All he could say was, 'Go, and the Lord be with you!'

At first Saul tried to put his own armour on David, but it was too large. Have you ever dressed up in your parents' clothes and found them much too big for you? So David went to fight against Goliath without any of Saul's armour.

He took his shepherd's staff in his hand, chose five smooth stones from a stream, put them in his bag, and with his sling in his hand, went towards Goliath.

Can you guess what the champion Goliath thought as he saw David? He looked David up and down, and saw he was only a boy. He thought him a nobody!

But David put a stone in his sling, and with one stone he struck the Philistine in the centre of his forehead, and he fell down on the ground - dead!

David - Mr. Nobody - became a champion, and later, David, Mr. Nobody, became a king.

There is a verse in the Bible which tells us that God deliberately chooses the no-bodies of this world to show people who think they are some-bodies how foolish they are to be so proud.

When we trust in God, and do what He wants, we can do things the world thinks impossible!

People who do not trust and obey God achieve little that lasts, even if they are thought important 'somebodies'. But all who trust and obey God can do great things to please Him and help others, even if the world thinks they are 'nobodies'!

No one is a Mr, Mrs, Master or Miss Nobody to God. The Lord Jesus, God's Son, taught that all of us are important to God, and He showed it by what He did. He left heaven, and came and lived in this world and died for ordinary people like us, who need a Saviour.

When we trust in the Lord Jesus as our Saviour, God makes us into people who are very special to Him. He makes those whom the world may think 'nobodies' into 'some-bodies' - people who can live to please Him.

Can you draw?

A picture of David fighting Goliath, with all the soldiers of both armies watching.

Where to read: 1 Samuel 16:1-13; 1 Samuel 17:1-51; 1 Corinthians 1:27

Mr **Obedient**

Obedience is something we all have to learn. What does it mean to be obedient? Yes, it means to do as we are told!

I wonder if you have ever had a puppy? One of the first things we try to teach a puppy is obedience. It is important that it should learn to do as it is told, not just for our sake but for its own. If it does not learn to obey, it may not do as it is told in dangerous traffic, and then perhaps be hurt or even run over.

To whom then should we be obedient? First, we should obey God. God gives us instructions and directions in His Word. As we do what He tells us in the Bible, we are obedient to Him.

To whom else should we be obedient? We should obey our parents and our teachers at school.

Let me tell you about Mr. Obedient. His real name was Ananias. There are three men called Ananias in the Acts of the Apostles. This is not the Ananias who sadly tried to lie to God and it is not the Ananias who was high priest. The Ananias who was Mr. Obedient lived in an important and busy city called Damascus.

He may not have lived there all his life because Christians moved to places like Damascus when they had to leave Jerusalem because of the persecution against Christians.

Something to do

Mark the map!
Find where Damascus is on page 46 and write in its name

16

Do you remember?

Persecution
see Our Bible dictionary, page 7

Our Bible dictionary

A Christian
People who believe in the Lord Jesus were first called Christians as a nick-name. Christians are those who belong to the Lord Jesus because they know that He died for their sins and rose again to be their Saviour and Lord.
It is another name for those who follow the Lord Jesus.

Conversion
To convert is to change, and conversion describes what happens when we become Christians: we turn from going our own way to going God's way. When we are converted, we turn from our sins, we believe in the Lord Jesus as our Saviour, and we want to spend the rest of our life pleasing the Lord Jesus who died and rose again for us.

Many Christians were ill-treated for their faith after the death of Stephen, one of the early Christians. The person behind the dreadful things that happened was Saul, who came from the town of Tarsus in Turkey. He went from house to house and dragged off men and women who believed in Jesus and put them in prison.

Ananias may have been one of the Christians who escaped from Jerusalem. Or he may have become a Christian through those believers who came to his city and witnessed about Jesus.

But something wonderful happened to Saul! He was on his way to Damascus to do there the dreadful things he had done to Christians in Jerusalem. But suddenly the Lord Jesus met Saul, and showed him that He was alive. Saul saw then that he had been wrong in all his thoughts about Jesus, and he was converted.

Saul understood for the first time why the Lord Jesus had come into the world. He believed now that He had died and risen again so that he - and people like us - might be forgiven and know God as Father. Saul became a Christian.

When Saul tried to open his eyes after meeting the Lord Jesus, he found that he could not see anything. So he had to be led by the hand to Damascus. For three days he was blind, and he did not eat or drink anything.

This was when Ananias proved himself to be Mr. Obedient.

The Lord Jesus spoke to Ananias in a vision. 'Ananias,' He called. Ananias replied, 'Yes, Lord.' That answer was important. Mr. Obedient is someone who calls Jesus 'Lord', and means it. Christians not only believe the Lord Jesus died for their sins, but they also know that He is God, the

Our Bible dictionary

Lord
Besides being the ordinary word to describe a person's boss or a slave's master, the word 'Lord' is a special name kept for God alone in the Bible. 'Lord' was the name or title the first followers of Jesus used when they spoke to Him or about Him. When we say 'Jesus is Lord' we are saying that He is God, and that He is worthy of our worship, service and obedience.

Lord, and the Person we ought always to obey. If we are Mr. or Miss Obedient, we will call Jesus 'Lord' too, and really mean it!

The Lord Jesus told Ananias, 'Go to Judas' house on Straight Street, and ask for a man from Tarsus, named Saul, and you will find him praying. In a vision he has seen a man named Ananias come and place his hands on him to restore his sight.'

Now Ananias - Mr. Obedient - thought this very difficult. 'Lord,' answered Ananias, 'I have heard many reports about this man and all the harm he has done to Your people in Jerusalem. And he has power and permission from the chief priests to arrest all who call on Your name.'

I can guess what Ananias was thinking. Saul had come to Damascus to arrest Christians and put them in prison, and here was the Lord Jesus telling

Ananias to go to him!

The Lord said to Ananias, 'Go! I have chosen this man to take My message to the nations and their kings, and to the Jewish people. I will show him how much he must suffer for My name.'

But Mr. Obedient wanted to obey, no matter how hard it might be. Ananias went because he was Mr. Obedient.

Whatever God says to us, we should do! And if we love the Lord Jesus, we will! God always wants to speak to us as we read His Word, the Bible, or listen to it being taught or preached at church and Sunday School. It will instruct us about things like honesty, respect for our parents, working hard at school, and many other good things. We please God when we gladly obey what His Word says.

Ananias went to Judas' house in Straight Street, where he found Saul. He placed his hands on him,

and said, 'Brother Saul, the Lord Jesus, who appeared to you on the road, has sent me so that you may see again, and be filled with the Holy Spirit.'

At once something like scales fell from Saul's eyes, and he could see again. He got up and showed his faith in the Lord Jesus by being baptised. Then he started eating again, and was strengthened.

Do you remember Ananias' first words to Saul? 'Brother Saul' was what he said. Ananias welcomed Saul into God's family, because he now trusted in the Lord Jesus. The people Saul had come to Damascus to persecute had become his brothers and sisters!

The name by which we best know Saul is Paul. He later became the famous apostle.

God has lots of good things and lovely surprises for those who obey Him.

We do not read of Ananias anywhere else in the Bible. He comes into this story about Saul and then he disappears. But he had done what God asked, and that is what Mr. Obedient always does.

The Lord Jesus said, 'If you love Me, keep My commandments.' All who love the Lord Jesus want to be Mr, Mrs, Master or Miss Obedient!

Where to read: Acts 9:1-19; John 14:15

Verses to look up

Fill in the blanks -

If we love the Lord Jesus we will:

o - - - what He commands (John 14:15).

l - - - one another (John 13:34).

l - - - our e - - - - - - (Matthew 5:44).

Mrs **Peacemaker**

D o you quarrel? I hope not. But all of us have to admit that we have sometimes quarrelled with others.

We may have said to a friend, 'I'm not going to speak to you again' or 'I'm not going to play with you any more.'

Have you ever tried to stop a fight or quarrel? When people quarrel they may refuse to speak to each other afterwards. They may even want to hurt or harm one another. Quarrels always make people unhappy.

The kind of person we need most when there are quarrels or arguments is a peacemaker. A peacemaker is someone who comes and helps us to try to make peace. That is what Mrs. Peacemaker did.

Her real name was Abigail. The Bible tells us she was both intelligent and beautiful. She was attrac-

tive not only in looks but also in character. But she had a husband who was quite the opposite. His name was Nabal, and he was sullen and grumpy, mean and stingy. He did not have many friends - perhaps even none - because he was so awkward and selfish.

Nabal was very wealthy and he possessed a thousand goats and three thousand sheep, and he employed many shepherds to look after them. Once his shepherds were looking for pasture for their flocks and they met David and his men. David was kind to them, and protected them from danger all the time they were with him.

One day David moved into the Desert of Maon,

Something to do

Mark the map!
Find where Maon is on the map on page 46 and write in its name.

near where Nabal and Abigail lived. David and his men needed food to eat. He remembered how he had met Nabal's shepherds in the desert and had helped them. So he sent ten young men and said to them, 'Go up to Nabal and greet him in my name. Say to him, "Long life to you! Good health to you and your household! And good health to all that is yours! Now I hear that it is sheep-shearing time. When your shepherds were with us, we did not ill-treat them, and the whole time they were with us nothing of theirs was missing. Ask your own servants and they will tell you. Therefore please be kind to my young men, and let them have any food that you can spare them." '

David's men went to Nabal and gave him David's message. Then they waited for his answer. They were in for a big surprise!

Nabal was rude and grumpy. He said to David's servants, 'Who is this David? Who is this son of Jesse? Why should I take my bread and water, and the meat I have prepared for my sheep shearers, and give it to men coming from who knows where? Be off with you!'

David's men turned round and went back. They told David everything Nabal had said. But then David made a big mistake. He decided to take revenge, and to have his own back. He said to his men, 'Put on your swords!' So they put them on, and David put on his. About four hundred men went up with David, while two hundred stayed behind. They were angry and furious because Nabal had been so unkind and unjust.

All would have gone sadly wrong if Mrs. Peacemaker had not acted. One of Nabal's servants told his wife, Abigail, 'David sent messengers from the desert to give our master his greetings, but he

insulted them. Yet David's men were very good to us. They did not ill-treat us when we were camped near them. They were like a wall of protection all around us. Please see if you can do anything, because disaster is hanging over our master and all of us. He is such a wicked man that no-one can talk to him!'

Abigail decided at once what she must do. It required great courage, and she lost no time. She took two hundred loaves of bread, two barrels of wine, five roasted sheep, seventeen kilogrammes of roasted grain, bunches of raisins and two hundred cakes of dried figs, and loaded them on donkeys.

Then she told her servants, 'Go on ahead; I'll follow you.' She did not tell her husband what she was doing because she knew he would have said 'No' and caused an even greater fuss.

As she was riding her donkey round a bend on a hillside, she met David and his men coming towards her. David had just been saying to his

Can you draw?

Draw Abigail meeting David, and include the donkeys carrying all the presents she took.

men, 'Nabal has paid me back evil for the good I tried to do his men. We will kill every man in his camp by morning.'

When Abigail saw David, she quickly got off her donkey and fell at his feet. She said, 'My lord, let the blame be on me alone. Please let your servant speak to you; hear what I have to say. Please pay no attention to what Nabal has said. I did not see the men you sent to my husband, otherwise I would have given them the food you need.'

She went on, 'I am glad that I have got to you in time before any fighting has begun. Please accept these gifts of food for the men who follow you. And please forgive my husband's behaviour, and do not have your own back. I know the Lord will fight for you, and give you success. Do not displease Him.'

As David listened to her, he knew she was right. He had been so angry that he had not thought how silly his plan to have his own back was. He said to Abigail, 'Praise be to the Lord, who has sent you to meet me today. Thank God for your good sense and what you had done in stopping me from taking revenge.'

Then David accepted the gifts of food for his men, and said to Abigail, 'Go home in peace. I will do what you say.'

Abigail - Mrs. Peacemaker - stopped David from taking revenge, which would have been a dreadful mistake. David knew he owed much to her, and he thanked God for her.

Abigail was right when she said that the Lord would fight for David against Nabal without David having to do anything. When Abigail returned home, Nabal was holding a party like that of a king. He was in high spirits and very drunk. So she told him nothing of what she had done until the morning. Then when he was sober, she told him everything, and the shock was so great that he had a stroke and was completely paralysed. He died ten days later.

How sad it would have been if David had gone against Nabal and killed him. He would then have been a murderer. The person who stopped him was Abigail, Mrs. Peacemaker.

The Bible has many encouraging words for peace-makers. The Lord Jesus says to us, 'Blessed are the peacemakers, for they will be called sons of God.' The Lord Jesus Himself came to be a peacemaker. That is why He died on the Cross. We have made ourselves God's enemies by our sin and our disobedience to His commandments. But He loves us so much that He sent the Lord Jesus to be the peacemaker, the One who could bring us back to God. The cost was great. The Lord Jesus took the punishment for our sins - including sins like quarrelling and fighting, and the pride that is so often behind them. God wants us to put our trust in the Lord Jesus as our Saviour, and then to live our lives following Him.

When the Lord Jesus is our Saviour, and we follow Him, we learn how to become peacemakers.

The world needs peacemakers. Families need peacemakers too. When we see people we know well quarrelling or arguing, we should try to be peacemakers.

God gives wisdom to those who believe in Jesus when they ask Him to make them peacemakers. Peacemakers please God, and they plant seeds of peace and reap a harvest of good things.

Where to read: 1 Samuel 25

Stop and think!

In which parts of the world are there wars and fighting today? Either now or when you go to bed tonight pray for peace, and for peace-makers to

Miss **Quizzer**

Something to do

Mark the map!
Find where Sheba
(modern Yemen) is on
the map on page 47
and write in its name.

Do you like quizzes? Lots of people do. That is why there are so many quiz programmes on television and radio, and quiz books for sale in bookshops.

I want us to think about Miss Quizzer, the Queen who asked questions!

We do not know her name, except that she was the Queen of Sheba. She was the ruler of the Sabeans, a people who were very powerful from about 900 to 450 BC.

Today we would call her country the Yemen, and it is one of the hottest and driest parts of the world.

She had questions because of all she had heard about King Solomon. He was the third king of Israel, and the son of King David. He was known as the richest king in the world. Most nations knew too about the great Temple he had built for God, and about his successful navy and army.

But it was not these things that particularly interested the Queen of Sheba, Miss Quizzer. She had heard too of the great wisdom God had given him.

Solomon's wisdom was God's special gift to him. It had happened like this. Soon after Solomon took his father David's place as king, the Lord appeared to Solomon during the night in a dream,

and said, 'Ask for whatever you want me to give you.'

Now Solomon could have asked to be wealthy and famous, but instead he asked to be made wise so that he could govern God's people properly.

God was pleased with Solomon, and said to him, 'Since you have asked for this and not for long life or wealth for yourself, I will do what you have asked. I will make you wiser than anyone has ever been, and I will give you too what you have not asked for - riches and honour.'

God always keeps His promises, and He gave Solomon wisdom to make good laws. Solomon was able to decide whether something was good or bad, fair or unfair, right or wrong.

God gave him wisdom to build magnificent buildings, and to plant beautiful gardens and parks. He was able to write poetry, and make up wise proverbs or sayings. There was no one as wise as Solomon in all the world!

When the Queen of Sheba heard about his wisdom, she did not believe anyone could be as wise as people said Solomon was. But the only way to find out the truth was to go and meet him, and ask him questions.

So off she went. It was a long journey on a camel of about 1,200 miles. As she travelled, she thought of all the hard questions she could ask Solomon. She probably asked some of the very wise and clever people of her own country to give her questions to ask. 'That question will beat him,' perhaps they said. 'Or if not that one, then this one will!'

Solomon made the Queen - Miss Quizzer - welcome when she arrived. She told him that she had heard about the wisdom God had given him, and she would like to ask him questions.

'Ask me whatever you would like to ask,' King Solomon said. And so she did! I expect she had a long list. But every question she asked, he answered perfectly. To even the most difficult questions, he knew the answers.

Lots of stories were told about Solomon's answers which are not in the Bible. We cannot be sure that they are true like the Bible, but they do show how everyone knew about Solomon's wisdom.

One story describes the final test the Queen made of Solomon's wisdom. Out in the palace garden she showed the king a bunch of the rarest and most beautiful flowers. They were not real

flowers, but artificial ones. They were so cleverly made that by looking at them no one could tell the difference from real flowers.

She deliberately did not let the king get close enough to smell them. She then asked him to tell her if they were real or artificial, not letting him hold them. I wonder what you would have done?

Some wild flowers were growing in the garden, and King Solomon said, 'Please put your bunch of flowers by those wild flowers.' And the queen did. The king had noticed a swarm of bees close by. They went to the wild flowers but none of the bees went near the artificial flowers because they could tell the difference!

'Your bunch of flowers is artificial,' said the King.

Miss Quizzer, the Queen of Sheba, was absolutely amazed at the King's wisdom. She said, 'The report I heard in my own country about your wisdom is true. I did not believe, but now I have seen it with my own eyes. The half was not told me. Praise be to the Lord your God who has placed you on the throne.'

Do you think anyone wiser than Solomon has lived in this world? Yes, the Lord Jesus Christ, God's Son.

People asked the Lord Jesus lots of questions. When the disciples did not understand the parables or stories Jesus told, they asked Him questions, and He gave the answers.

Some people asked Jesus questions to try to catch Him out, but they always failed. The Lord Jesus knew not only their questions, but what was going on in their minds and hearts.

You and I often have questions, and it is good to ask questions when we do not understand some-

Something sad!

Although Solomon began well by asking God for wisdom, there came a time when he foolishly turned from God and worshipped idols. Perhaps he had become proud of his wisdom because of all the praise it brought him. But whatever the reason, turning away from God, he then spoiled the wonderful gift of wisdom God had given him, and he made sad mistakes in his life.

thing.

I can think of lots of questions I have had. I wonder if you have had some of the same ones? Why is there wrong and evil in the world? How are we different from animals and other creatures? Why did God make us? Why did the Lord Jesus have to die upon the Cross if we were to be forgiven our sins?

Miss Quizzer - the Queen of Sheba - had to travel to the King's palace in Jerusalem to get her answers because God had given His wisdom to Solomon.

We do not have to travel a long way to find our answers. God has given us His Book, the Bible, which tells us about the life and teaching of the Lord Jesus, the one Person who can give answers to our most important questions.

The Bible promises that those who seek find. The Queen of Sheba really wanted to know the truth about Solomon's wisdom, and she found out the truth.

When we really want to find out the truth about the Lord Jesus from the Bible, we always discover it, and the Lord Jesus gives the right answers to the most important questions we ever ask.

Where to read: 1 Samuel 25 1 Kings 10 1-13
2 Chron 9 1-12.

33

Mr **Runaway**

A runaway is someone who runs away from home, usually without telling anyone where he or she is going.

I hope you have never thought of running away from home! Or perhaps from school! But if you ever have, I think I can guess what made you feel like it. It was probably when you did something wrong, and you were afraid of what might happen to you!

The person we are calling Mr. Runaway was a young man called Onesimus. Can you say that name? It is an unusual one, and it means 'useful'. That was a good name for him because he was a slave.

Slaves did not control their own lives, but instead belonged to other people, whom they called their 'masters'.

Unfortunately, slavery was common in the first century throughout the Roman empire.

People became slaves in different ways. Some were born slaves, because their parents were slaves.

Sometimes parents felt they could not look after their children when they were born, and they simply left them on the streets, and they were brought up slaves.

People who were poor even sold their children as

slaves. Others became slaves to pay their debts. Some were kidnapped and then forced to be slaves.

We do not know how Onesimus became a slave, but Roman laws gave his master great power over him. His master's name was Philemon and he lived in a place called Colosse.

Fortunately for Onesimus his master was a Christian. But that did not stop Onesimus running away.

Onesimus did something wrong. We do not know what it was, but it must have been something very bad.

Now when we do something bad, we usually deserve to get into trouble, don't we?

Onesimus decided to run away. It seems likely that he stole some of his master's possessions, perhaps to pay for the journey.

He travelled as fast as he could, and he made for a big city. It was either Ephesus or Rome. Ephesus was not far from Colosse, but it was large enough to get lost in. Rome was a much larger place - like London

or New York - where many runaways went because they thought they would be able to hide there.

Someone we know about was in prison in the city at the time - it was the apostle Paul. Paul was not a prisoner because of wrong he had done, but because some people did not want him to preach the good news about Jesus.

We do not know how Onesimus met Paul, but he did. Perhaps Onesimus was arrested, and found himself put in the same cell as Paul.

What do you think Paul wanted to talk about most of all with Onesimus? I am sure he wanted to tell him the good news about the Lord Jesus.

He said something like this to him, 'Onesimus, even though you have done wrong, God loves you. You have hurt not only your master, Philemon, but you have sinned against God. But the good news for you and me is that the Lord Jesus, God's Son, died for sinners, for people like us.'

Paul explained to Onesimus that he could be forgiven, if he was really sorry for what he had done, and put his trust in the Lord Jesus as his Saviour.

And that is just what Onesimus did! There in prison with Paul he received the Lord Jesus into his life as his Saviour, and all his sins were forgiven. How glad and grateful Onesimus was!

He then tried to help Paul in any way he could. He looked after him just as a son might care for his father. He became like his name - useful.

But one day Paul said, 'Onesimus, you must go back to your master. It is not right that you should look after me when you are really Philemon's slave.'

Onesimus was afraid about going back, because Philemon had great powers over him. Having run

Something to do

Mark the map!
Find where Rome, Ephesus and Colosse are on the map on page 47 and write in their names.

37

away, he deserved even to be put to death according to Roman law.

Paul understood Onesimus' fears, and he also knew his master Philemon well. 'I'll write a letter for you,' Paul said. The letter went like this, 'I appeal to you for Onesimus, who has become a Christian, and like a son to me here in prison. Once he was useless to you, but now he has become useful both to you and to me. I am sending him back to you. I would have liked to keep him with me so that he could take your place in helping me while I am in prison. But I did not want to do anything without your permission. I did not want you to be kind because you had to but because you wanted to. Perhaps the reason he was separated from you for a little while was that you might have him back for good - no longer as a slave, but better than a slave, as a dear brother. He is very dear to me, but even dearer to you, both as a man and as a brother in the Lord. So if you consider me a friend, welcome him as you would welcome me. If he has done you any wrong or owes you anything, charge it to me.' That was a good letter for Onesimus to carry back to Colosse!

Onesimus had run away because he had done wrong, and was afraid.

He learned that it is impossible to run away from God because God is everywhere.

He discovered too that when we trust in the Lord Jesus as our Saviour, He teaches us not to run away from hard or difficult tasks and duties.

We may often be tempted to run away from something we ought to do. It is always silly, and it never works!

Sometimes people even try to run away from

God! We cannot do that, because He sees and knows what we are doing wherever we are. If we try to run away from God, we run from the only One who can really help us. Onesimus discovered that.

God always helps runaways when they decide to do what is right. God gave Mr. Runaway Paul's help, both in the prison and in the letter he wrote to Philemon for him.

When do you think Onesimus was happier - when he was running away from his master because he was afraid, or when he was going back to Colosse as a Christian with Paul's letter in his hand?

When we trust in the Lord Jesus, we discover we can be really happy only when we do what is right, and that is the lesson Mr. Runaway, Onesimus, learned. It is an important lesson for us too. When we want to do the right thing the Lord Jesus is always with us to help us.

Where to read: Philemon 1-25

Mr **Sulker**

Something to do

Mark the map!
Find where Jezreel is on the map on page 46 and write in its name.

What do we mean when we say that people are sulking? We usually mean that they are cross and angry about something. When people sulk they may lose their temper or refuse to talk to anyone.

They may look sullen, miserable, cross and perhaps even pout. They may throw things on the ground or go into their bedroom and shut the door on everyone.

Have you seen anyone sulk? I wonder if you have ever sulked? It is not pleasant for other people when someone sulks. It usually makes others unhappy.

It is not only children who sulk, but grown up people too. The Bible tells about a king who sulked. His name was King Ahab. He was not a good king. Instead of worshipping the Lord Jehovah, the one true God, he worshipped false gods.

He foolishly married a wicked woman called Jezebel who encouraged him to worship her gods. He listened to her far more than he listened to God. God sent His prophet Elijah to tell Ahab what he ought to do, but he refused to listen.

King Ahab had a summer palace in Jezreel. One day he was looking out of his palace, and he noticed a fruitful vineyard nearby. It was close to a spring of water which kept everything green and

attractive. He thought to himself, 'That would make a lovely vegetable garden.'

The vineyard belonged to a man called Naboth, and the land had belonged to him, and his forefathers, for many many years.

King Ahab decided to speak to Naboth about it, and so he went to see him. He said, 'Let me have your vineyard to use for a vegetable garden, since it is close to my palace. In exchange I will give you a better vineyard or, if you prefer, I will pay you whatever it is worth.'

But Naboth knew he had to say 'no', and for a very good reason. 'I cannot let you have it,' replied

Naboth, 'no matter how much you might be willing to give me for it. This land is what the Lord gave to my father, and his father before him - and longer ago than that - and I must look after it, and leave it to my children when I die.'

That was a good and right reason for not wanting to sell the land.

Ahab was not at all pleased, and he showed it. He returned home, sullen and angry. He refused to talk to anyone, and went straight to his bedroom. He lay on his bed sulking and would not eat anything. And he was a king and a grown man!

Jezebel, his wife, found him, and asked, 'What on earth is wrong? Why aren't you eating? What has made you so angry and upset?'

'I asked Naboth to sell me his vineyard, or to exchange it for some other land, and he refused!' Ahab complained miserably.

'Is this how you act as a king?' asked Jezebel. 'Get up! Don't worry about it. You have something to eat, and I'll take care of Naboth and get you his vineyard.'

And she did! But she did something very nasty and wrong. She arranged for two men who would do anything bad if they were paid for it to accuse Naboth of cursing God and the king. That was a very serious crime. Of course, Naboth had done nothing of the sort, but the men in charge of the city of Jezreel did what Jezebel wanted, and they dragged Naboth out of the city and stoned him to death.

When Jezebel heard the news, she said to King Ahab, who was still sulking, 'Get up and take possession of Naboth's vineyard, which he refused to sell you. He is no longer alive, but dead.'

Instead of asking what had happened to Naboth

or being sad that Naboth had died, King Ahab got up and went down to take possession of Naboth's vineyard. He was not sulking any more, now he was pleased.

But God was not pleased. Soon God sent His prophet Elijah to Ahab to tell him that He knew all about his sulking and what had happened to Naboth.

God does not like us sulking because sulking means we are thinking of ourselves rather than others - and that is selfishness. God does not like sulking because it often shows that we are not happy with what we already have.

But most of all He does not like sulking because it is the opposite of our being like the Lord Jesus Christ.

True or False?

Place a 'T' where true, and a 'F' where false against these sentences:

When we sulk we are happy.

When we sulk we look miserable.

When we sulk people like to be with us.

When we sulk we are thinking of ourselves rather than others.

We do not please God when we sulk.

The Lord Jesus never sulked; instead, He was always kind, loving, pleasant and unselfish, and that is what God wants us to be like. When we trust the Lord Jesus as our Saviour, and He lives in us by His Spirit, He teaches us not to sulk.

Do we sulk? If we do, is it because we do not know the Lord Jesus as our Saviour? Or is it because we are not listening to God's Spirit when He tells us that He wants us to be like Jesus?

When we are tempted to sulk we should remember the bad example of King Ahab - Mr. Sulker - and the horrible effects it had on others.

Where to read: 1 Kings 21:1-19

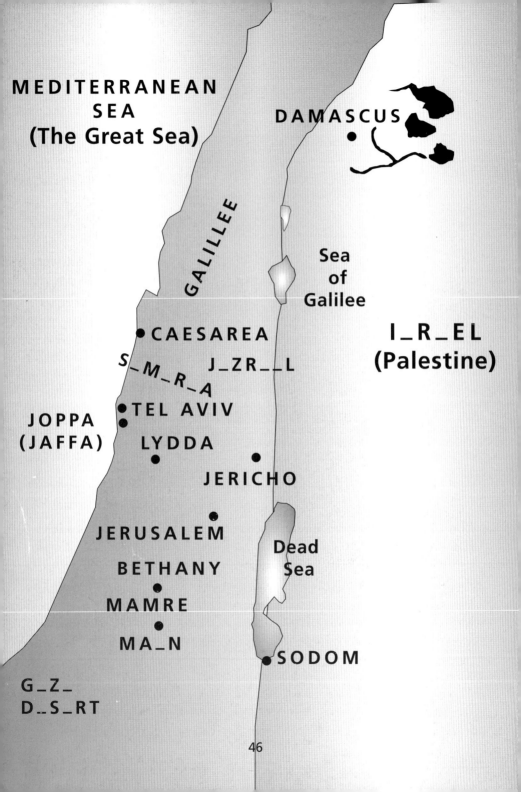

MEDITERRANEAN
SEA
(The Great Sea)

DAMASCUS

GALILLEE

Sea
of
Galilee

I_R_EL
(Palestine)

● CAESAREA

S_M_R_A

J_ZR__L

● TEL AVIV

JOPPA
(JAFFA)

LYDDA

● JERICHO

● JERUSALEM

BETHANY

Dead
Sea

MAMRE

MA_N

● SODOM

G_Z_
D_S_RT

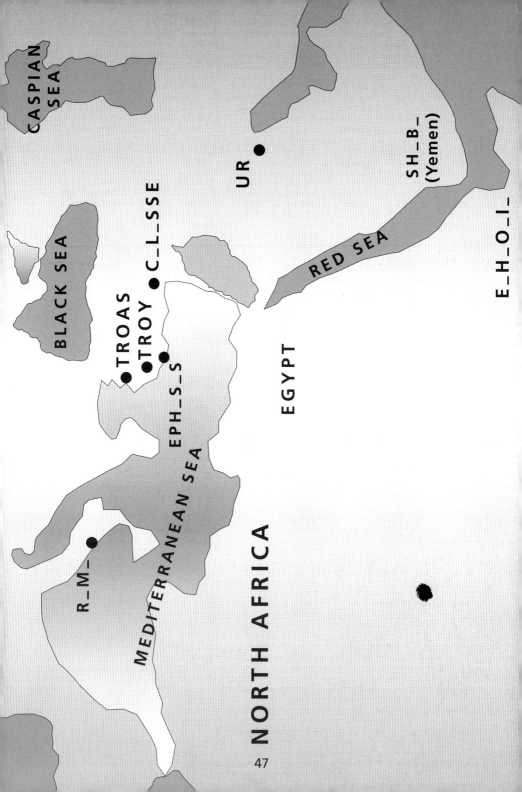

CASPIAN SEA

BLACK SEA

UR

SH_B_
(Yemen)

RED SEA

E_H_O_I_

TROAS

TROY

C_L_SSE

EPH_S_S

EGYPT

MEDITERRANEAN SEA

R_M_

NORTH AFRICA

47